JESUS CHRIST
IS
PERFECT THEOLOGY

Edited by Frank A. DeCenso Jr.

DESTINY IMAGE PUBLISHERS

© Copyright 2009 – Frank DeCenso Jr.

All rights reserved. This book is protected by the copyright laws of the United States of America. This book may not be copied or reprinted for commercial gain or profit. The use of short quotations or occasional page copying for personal or group study is permitted and encouraged. Permission will be granted upon request. Unless otherwise noted, Scripture quotations are taken from the New King James Version. Copyright © 1982 by Thomas Nelson, Inc. Used by permission. All rights reserved. Scripture quotations marked AMP are from the Amplified® Bible, Copyright © 1954, 1958, 1962, 1964, 1965, 1987 by The Lockman Foundation. Used by permission. Scripture quotations marked NASB are from the NEW AMERICAN STANDARD BIBLE®, Copyright © 1960, 1962, 1963, 1968, 1971, 1972, 1973, 1975, 1977, 1995 by The Lockman Foundation. Used by permission. Scripture quotations marked NLT are from the Holy Bible, New Living Translation, copyright © 1996, 2004. Used by permission of Tyndale House Publishers, Wheaton, IL 60189. All rights reserved. Scripture quotations marked NRSV are from the New Revised Standard Version of the Bible, copyright © 1989 by the Division of Christian Education of the National Council of the Churches of Christ in the U.S.A.; used by permission. Scripture quotations marked NIV are taken from the NEW INTERNATIONAL VERSION®, Copyright 1973, 1978, 1984 International Bible Society. Used by permission of Zondervan. All rights reserved. Scripture quotations marked KJV are taken from the King James Version. Emphasis within Scripture is the authors' own. Please note that Destiny Image's publishing style capitalizes certain pronouns in Scripture that refer to the Father, Son, and Holy Spirit, and may differ from some publishers' styles. Take note that the name satan and related names are not capitalized. We choose not to acknowledge him, even to the point of violating grammatical rules.

DESTINY IMAGE® PUBLISHERS, INC.

P.O. Box 310, Shippensburg, PA 17257-0310

"Speaking to the Purposes of God for this Generation

and for the Generations to Come."

This book and all other Destiny Image, Revival Press, Mercy Place, Fresh Bread, Destiny Image Fiction, and Treasure House books are available at Christian bookstores and distributors worldwide.

For a U.S. bookstore nearest you, call 1-800-722-6774.

For more information on international availability, call 717-532-3040.

Reach us on the Internet at www.destinyimage.com.

Digital Edition ISBN: 978-0-7684-1397-7

Trade Paper ISBN 13: 978-0-7684-1620-6

Originally published in *Amazed by the Power of God*, ISBN 978-0-7684-2755-4.

Jesus Christ
is
Perfect Theology

Bill Johnson

JESUS CHRIST IS PERFECT THEOLOGY

Jesus Christ is perfect theology. Whatever you think you know about God that you can't find in the person of Jesus, you have a reason to question. Jesus Christ is the precise revelation of the nature of the Father. As Jesus is manifested to us in Scripture, so we are to present Him to this world. Revelation makes us responsible and accountable, for He said to us, "As the Father has sent Me, I also send you" (John 20:21).

Early in life through the Christmas message we hear the angels proclaim, "Glory to God in the highest, and on earth peace, *goodwill toward men!*" (Luke 2:14). This is God's heart toward humanity. It's the message that introduced Jesus to the world and must remain the message that introduces the Church to the world.

Believers easily say, "Yes, God is good." We have to; the Bible says so. But when tragedy strikes, many say, "I know He's good, but His ways are mysterious," thinking that God causes evil because He'll work it out for good in the end. The implication is that God sometimes brings crises, disease, and torment to teach us to be better Christians. There is no question that God can work good out of evil. This is a testimony to His greatness, and His redemptive purpose in our lives. But to attribute evil to Him tragically undermines our purpose on the earth, as it cripples our ability to *re*-present Jesus as the manifestation of God's *goodwill toward all*. Furthermore it compromises our ability to discern the difference between God's discipline and actual demonic assault.

Conflict often arises when discussing the nature of God's goodness. The portrayal of God "as one who afflicts" usually has an old covenant Scripture as its proof text. It is wrong to take an Old Testament revelation of God, of His nature, and preempt or trump the New Testament revelation of God found in Jesus Christ. Inferior covenants do not provide clearer insights into the nature of God. Scripture is Scripture. All of it was written for our instruction. But what is observed in the Law and the Prophets does not possess the clarity that is found in the person of Jesus.

Purpose for the Old Testament

There are countless benefits of the Old Testament Scriptures for the New Testament believer. But improper use of them has impaired many a Christian's life. Here are at least three beneficial uses.

1. The Old Testament gives us an awareness of our sinfulness. The apostle Paul explains it, "...where there is no law there is no transgression" (Rom. 4:15).

2. The Old Testament Law is the tutor that leads us to Christ. "Therefore the Law has become our *tutor* to lead us to Christ, so that we may be justified by faith. But now that faith has come,

we are no longer under a *tutor*" (Gal. 3:24-25 NASB).

3. In that the Old Testament leads us to Jesus, it naturally portrays this King in His Kingdom. Throughout the time before Christ, there were events, prophecies, and laws that spoke of life under grace. There were unusual moments of grace that gave insight into what was coming through "types and shadows."

Wonderful revelations are gained from the Old Testament through types and shadows. For example, we know that the Jews sacrificed a spotless lamb at the temple as a payment for their sin. But we also know that Jesus is the actual Lamb of God who takes away the sin of the world. Once fulfillment comes to the Old Testament type or symbol, there's no more need to go back and embrace the shadow.

The new covenant reveals the Father clearly in the person of Jesus Christ. Jesus said, "If you've seen Me, you've seen the Father" (see John 14:9). Hebrews declares, "God, after He spoke long ago to the fathers in the prophets in many portions and in many ways, in these last days has spoken to us in His Son" (Heb. 1:1-2 NASB). Furthermore, He is "the exact representation of His nature." God is now speaking primarily through the person and work of Jesus. The two are exactly alike. That is what is so *new* about the New Testament—God is seen clearly in Jesus.

The entire Old Testament points to Jesus. He is the central figure of Scripture. The Law and the Prophets declare His role as Messiah and assure us that Jesus is the One—the fulfillment of God's redemptive plan. The stories, prophecies, and laws all point to Him at various levels in the same way a highway sign points to an upcoming city. The sign is real and significant. But in itself it is not the reality we are looking for. It points to something greater than itself. In this case we must not worship the sign of the Old Testament. It serves its purpose by taking us to the Messiah Himself. A freeway sign never defines the city itself, and neither should the Old Testament redefine who Jesus is. He is the fulfillment of both the Law and the Prophets. The nature of His life and purpose is clear—He came to *destroy* the works of the devil.

There is a deep personal need in the Body of Christ to see Jesus for who He is. Jesus healed everyone who came to Him. That doesn't change because not everyone I pray for gets healed. He stilled every life-threatening storm that He encountered. And deliverance came to all who asked. This is Jesus. And this is the Father, exactly.

There is a vast difference between the goodness of God seen in the life of Jesus and the goodness of God revealed in the Church because of our present-day beliefs. It has become easier to believe either that the standard Jesus set for our lives is entirely unattainable or that it is theologically wrong to consider it a legitimate standard for today. It is far too difficult for many to reconcile the differences in the life of Jesus and the experience of the everyday believer; so bad theology is created. It's sometimes easier to change our interpretation of the intent of Scripture than it is to seek God until He answers.

If Jesus healed everyone who came to Him, and the Father wills people to be sick, then we have a divided house—one that according to Jesus cannot stand. Invariably it's at this point in the discussion that people bring up Old Testament verses in an attempt to prove the point that God causes sickness. I can't think of an area other than miracles, signs, and wonders, which would include prophecy, that the Church does this with. We would never endorse the sacrifice of an actual lamb to atone for sin even though the Old Testament gave the command. Nor would we make people travel to Jerusalem so they can be involved in acceptable worship to God. These things we would never do. But we do the equivalent to the subject of healing. If an Old Testament Scripture supersedes the perfect revelation of God in Christ on the subject of healing, we have illegally taken license to redefine the nature of the Kingdom. We do this with no other part of the gospel.

Two thousand years ago Jesus considered all sickness to be from the devil, and healing was a sign of God's Kingdom come. Even something as simple as a fever was considered to be of the devil. (See Mark 1:31.) Things have disintegrated so far that many consider sickness to be sent or allowed by God to build our character. Those who pursue healing are thought to be out of balance at best, and from the devil at worst. It's frightening to see how far things can fall in 2,000 years. What is even more puzzling is that the very ones who consider the sickness to be approved by God for our benefit have no problem going to the doctor to find a cure and release from disease. Such mindless approaches to Scripture must stop.

Believing that God is good is absolutely vital to becoming effective in the ministry of the gospel. Without that foundation, it's not possible to develop the clear focus and the strength of faith to pursue the breakthroughs that the earth aches for. The way we understand Him is the way we will present Him. How we see Him defines how we think and how we live.

I am not saying that God doesn't discipline. When I talk about the goodness of God and the greatness of Jesus and His grace and His kindness, I don't forget that He was also the one who chased the moneychangers out of the temple with a whip. It's just that He does not use sickness, any more than He uses sin, to discipline His children. If I did to my children what many Christians claim God does to His, I'd be arrested for child abuse.

When we understand the nature of God, we see that Jesus is not warring against the Father to reveal a different standard. He is perfectly representing and manifesting the nature of the Father. This is a big deal because in the back of the minds of so many people is a picture of the Father willing certain calamities and difficulties and Jesus interceding, trying to talk Him out of it. While very few will put it in that language, it is the imagery that is behind much of how the Church lives and thinks. Insurance companies and newspapers call natural disasters "an act of God." Where did they get their theology? From us.

We don't ever find Jesus blessing a storm that was coming at Him and the disciples. He never redirected the storm, saying, "Go to that city; destroy them. It will teach them how to pray. They will become more like Me." On the contrary, He stilled the storm. He rebuked His disciples for wanting to call down fire on people, saying, "You don't know what spirit you are of." (See Luke 9:54.) We never see Him using His authority to increase a storm or to bring calamity of any kind. We always see Him bringing an end to a storm or sickness. Regardless of how or why the storm came about, Jesus was the solution.

We can either create a doctrine that allows for lack, or seek God until He answers. When the disciples didn't get a miracle breakthrough, they asked Jesus why. In other words, they expected breakthrough. An environment of expectation naturally creates a desire to find out "why" when a breakthrough doesn't come. Today it's easier to blame God than to accept the fact that we're the ones He left in charge.

The Nature of the Message

"The Law and the Prophets were proclaimed until John; since that time the gospel of the kingdom of God has been preached, and everyone is forcing his way into it" (Luke 16:16 NASB).

"Until John" is a significant phrase, but one that is nearly forgotten. Both the Law and the Prophets were superseded by another message, the gospel of the Kingdom. One still exists; the other has become obsolete. One has Heaven's backing; the other doesn't. One reveals our assignment; the other does not.

A message creates a reality. The nature of the message determines the nature of the reality in which we will live and minister. The

Kingdom message creates an environment suitable to the display of God's love, purity, and power. It is the message that Jesus preached and in turn taught His disciples to preach. It is the *now word.*

The Church has largely replaced the gospel of the Kingdom with the gospel of salvation. The gospel of salvation is focused on getting people saved and going to Heaven. The beauty of that message makes it very easy to miss the fact that it is only a part of the whole message that Jesus gave us. The gospel of the Kingdom is focused on the transformation of lives, cities, and nations, bringing the reality of Heaven to earth. We must not confuse our destiny with our assignment. *Heaven is my destiny, while bringing the Kingdom is my assignment.* The focus of the Kingdom message is the rightful dominion of God over everything.

Whatever is inconsistent with Heaven, namely disease, torment, sin habits, etc., must come under the authority of the King. These kinds of issues must be dealt with and broken off of people's lives because these inferior realms cannot stand wherever the dominion of God is realized. As we succeed in displaying this message, we are positioned to bring about cultural change in business, politics, the environment, and essential issues that face us today. This creates a most unusual phenomenon: the fruit of revival becomes the fuel of revival, which produces the fruit of revival, etc. It is circular, unto reformation.

When Heaven Was Silent

Why did Jesus say, "until John"? Why didn't He say, "until Jesus"? Because John was the one who broke Heaven's silence with the message of the Kingdom. Before John the Baptist came on the scene, there were 400 years without one word from God. Heaven was silent. No visions, dreams, or prophecies. Nothing. Four hundred years of absolute silence, and then came John. The Holy Spirit is not carelessly highlighting this detail that the Law and the Prophets were until John because it was John who first declared, "Repent, for the Kingdom of Heaven is at hand" (Matt. 3:2).

There is another place in Scripture where 400 years is unusually significant. Understanding the first mention of this phrase, *400 years*, will help us to understand its significance in this case. Israel was a nation of slaves, living in Egypt for 400 years. And then everything changed in a moment. The blood from a lamb was put on the doorpost of each Jewish home on the Passover (see Exod. 12:23). The Angel of the Lord came and released the Jews from their slavery to Egypt. In one moment, they went from being slaves, to being free, from absolute poverty, to possessing the wealth of the most prosperous nation in the world. It happened in a moment. The first mention of the phrase *400 years* in the Bible resulted in the rescue and creation of a new nation, the redemption of God's people. In the time of John, God announces a rescue and creation of a new nation declaring, "It's a new day!"

That is exactly the message of Jesus in Luke 16:16. It's a new day! The new day is marked with a new message. One message is over, and another has begun. When John the Baptist came forth, it was even more significant than deliverance from 400 years of slavery under

Egypt. This deliverance dealt with the nature and potential of humankind. John's pronouncement changed everything.

Jesus made the amazing statement, "Now the Kingdom of God is being preached and *everyone is pressing into it*" (see Luke 16:16). Is it possible that the nature of the message determines the size of the harvest? He did say, *everyone!* This is the message: "Jesus is Lord over all. His dominion is everlasting. It is now!" When you declare the right message, you create an atmosphere where everyone is able to press in. No matter the need, there is an answer. The right message capitalizes on the truth that Jesus is called *The Desire of the Nations*. The right message changes the atmosphere to make the manifestation of His dominion realized. Perhaps this is the context in which the irresistible grace of God is embraced, thus fulfilling the desire born in the heart of every person alive.

It Is Finished

After this, Jesus, knowing that all things were now accomplished, that the Scripture might be fulfilled, said, "I thirst!" ... So when Jesus had received the sour wine, He said, ***"It is finished!"*** *And bowing His head, He gave up His spirit* (John 19:28,30).

It is a mistake to think that when Jesus cried out, "It is finished," He was merely proclaiming that His life as a human being was over. He came to quench the appetite of an unquenchable fire by satisfying the demands of the Law and the Prophets. When He said, "It is finished," He was declaring, "The appetite of the Law and Prophets has been satisfied. It's a new day. It is finished." We go from a slave to a possessor of the Kingdom in a moment: from being the one who has no right in God to suddenly being the eternal dwelling place of God Himself.

Repenting Enough to See the Kingdom

"Repent, for the Kingdom of Heaven is at hand." One of the ways I like to illustrate this is in Hebrews 6:1, "Repentance *from* dead works...faith *toward* God." Full repentance is *from* something *toward* something—*from* sin *toward* God. Many Christians repent enough to be forgiven but not enough to see the Kingdom. Their repentance doesn't bring the Kingdom into view. Jesus tells us to repent because He brought His world with Him. If I don't shift my perspective on reality, I will never discover that which is superior—the unseen realm of His dominion.

Luke writes it this way: "Repent therefore and be converted, that your sins may be blotted out, so that times of refreshing may come from the presence of the Lord" (Acts 3:19). The point is: *the presence is the Kingdom.* It's too easy to over-complicate the Christian life. We are told to put on the full armor of God, which includes the helmet of salvation, breastplate of righteousness, and so on (see Eph. 6:10-18). The apostle Paul gave us this important instruction, but most of us miss the point. God is my armor. He's not saying, "Put something on that is a reality that is separate from Me." He's saying, "I'm it. Just abide in Me. I become your salvation. I am your righteousness, the breastplate over you. I am the gospel of peace. I am the good news. I am the sword of the Spirit." This list is a profound word picture enabling us to realize the fuller benefit of abiding in Christ.

The Kingdom is about discovering presence, the person of the Lord Jesus Christ. Why? He's the message. He's perfect theology. We can't defile or distort the message of who He is so that we can accommodate something that took place in the days of an inferior covenant. To try to reactivate the voice of the Law and Prophets, and let it trump and overtake the clear manifestation of the nature of God found in Jesus, is theologically immoral.

Releasing His Presence

Remember when Jesus sent the disciples out two by two? He told them to go into a home, let their peace rest on that home, and if there was not a person of peace there, they should take the peace back and leave. (See Luke 10:5-7.) That was vital ministry instruction that most of us know little about. In order to understand this issue, we need a stronger awareness of our relationship with the Holy Spirit.

There is an Old Testament type and shadow of the Holy Spirit descending as a dove in the story of Noah. He released the dove to find out if there was any dry land. When the dove could find no place to rest, the dove returned to Noah. Every time you talk and you declare Kingdom realities, you release the Holy Spirit.

And He is looking for a life to rest upon. Learning how that presence is released is essential in ministry. I find that the same thing happens when we are with people who have a genuine hunger for the Kingdom. They actually draw upon the Spirit within us. That is how Jesus knew that power went out from Him when the woman touched the edge of His garment (see Mark 5:30). He carried such an awareness of the Holy Spirit upon Him that He felt power being released.

As we speak, His presence is released. He is always looking for another person to rest upon. This is their call and summons into their eternal purpose as the dwelling place of God, and as a broker of His dominion. When we talk about the Kingdom of God being at hand, we are talking about the presence of the Almighty God. You cannot separate presence and Kingdom.

Our ministry *is* the release of presence. It is why we say what He is saying because as we speak, our words define the ministry of the Spirit of God that is being released and manifested into the environment. We are called and assigned by God to stand within society and bring the Word of the Lord. We are even told of a day coming when the nations of the world will stream to us seeking the word of the Lord (see Micah 4:2).

A Word Born in Courage

An expression of the *dunamis* power released on the Church at Pentecost is courage. Courage enables us to speak with a boldness that God says "Amen" to. Declaring His word requires courage. And manifesting His will is our intentional response to the word we just declared that requires risk. Much of what is preached today is without boldness. If Jesus had preached what was preached in most pulpits on any given Sunday, He never would have been crucified.

"*And they went out and preached everywhere, the Lord working with them, confirming the word through the accompanying signs*" (Mark 16:19). Much of what is presently taught and confessed by the Church can be accomplished apart from

God. Most of it appeals to human talent and skill. Whatever we can do for God is important but secondary to what we've been called to do that is impossible. The ability to rally the people of God together and work hard to accomplish a project for the Lord will never satisfy our inner longing to see impossibilities bend their knee to the name of Jesus.

But the Lord is stirring up a courage that is anchored to eternal purpose. In Acts 4:29-30, Peter had just gotten out of prison; he had just suffered persecution for the name of Jesus, yet he was ready to take it up a notch. He said, "Lord, please take note of their threats and grant that Your bondservants could preach Your word with all boldness." He asked God to increase his boldness: the very thing that got him in trouble. The Lord is looking for a word that is born in courage, so that He *has* to show up to confirm it. May the Lord give us a word that confronts the powers of darkness, releases Heaven on earth, and launches people into their God-born destinies: something to which God can say "Amen."

We are a people chosen by God to declare what God is saying, releasing the presence of the Lord all over the earth. This was all His idea—that the glory of the Lord would cover the earth as the water covers the sea, and there would be no end to the increase of His government. You and I are servants in bringing the kingdoms of this world into His domain, where the presence of God is seen in every aspect and area of life.

The Power of Righteousness

Societal transformation is not an accidental by-product of revival. It is to be intentional. In revival the Church becomes more convinced of a big God than a big devil. Such a shift in focus changes what's possible. But it's our internal world that is the first thing to change in the glory of His outpouring. For such a transformation to take place in the world around us, it must first happen to the world within us. Only what is true on the inside can be released to the outside. Jesus conquered a storm with peace. It was the storm He slept in. The peace that kept Him in rest was the peace that delivered Him from the storm itself. Internal realities become our external realities. That is the nature of ministry: living from the inside out.

Without the outpouring of the Spirit, the Church becomes more concerned with being contaminated by evil than we do of contaminating the world with righteousness. While we should never take sin lightly, neither should we be ignorant of the power of holiness.

Much of our present view of the world is built on Old Testament revelation. It's not wrong; it's just incomplete. If I lived under Jewish law before Christ, and I offered a sacrifice to the Lord, but on the way to the temple someone who was unclean touched my offering, the offering would have become unclean. Sin affects. That's why touching a leper made a person unclean. The emphasis in the old covenant revelation was that sin is powerful. It destroys whatever it touches.

Things are different in the New Testament. The Gospel of Matthew was written primarily for the Jews. In his account of Jesus' life, Matthew mentioned Jesus touching the leper as the first miracle. When He touched the leper, the leper became clean. This testimony confronted an incomplete mindset that was not adequate for His present work of grace on the earth. The power of holiness becomes even clearer when we read that a believing spouse sanctifies the entire unbelieving household. This Kingdom mindset requires a shift in how we view and value life itself and the effect of the life of Christ in us. Faith in Kingdom realities manifests Kingdom realities.

The power of holiness becomes clearer in the story of Daniel. God took Daniel and allowed him to be numbered with witches and warlocks before King Nebuchadnezzar. He lived righteously and brought about a New Testament effect of holiness and loyalty on an entire kingdom until that ungodly leader was converted. Holiness is more powerful than sin; it's the purity of Christ in you.

Highway of Holiness

There is an environment created in the outpouring of the Spirit where holiness becomes the natural by-product. Isaiah speaks of the highway of holiness. A highway is a road designed to expedite travel, where obstacles have been removed. It usually involves easy access and fellow travelers. A highway of holiness builds momentum for the people of God to live in purity. It is so significant that even foolish things get covered. It's not to call for, allow for, or encourage foolish things. Many living righteously create a momentum where even the weak succeed.

*A highway shall be there, and a road,
And it shall be called the Highway of
Holiness.*

The unclean shall not pass over it,
But it shall be for others.
Whoever walks the road, although a fool,
Shall not go astray (Isaiah 35:8).

This Highway of Holiness will not be known for compromise. You won't have people who outwardly pretend to be holy but inwardly are corrupt. "Whoever walks the road, although a fool, shall not go astray" means that God is creating such a highway in this time of outpouring that it's going to be hard to wander off the road. This concept is difficult for many to receive as we are accustomed to the opposite. We are quick to speak about the "great falling away," but not the great harvest and city transformation that is also a part of end-time prophecy. A day is coming when there will exist a righteous peer pressure, without the fear of man.

New Testament theology emphasizes the power of holiness, not the power of sin. It's not that we shouldn't fear sin. It remains powerful. But a shift in focus will position us to invade the world instead of requiring the world to come to us.

I remember being taught that holiness was a list of things you can and can't do—and the "can't do" list was longer than the "can do" list. Mostly what was on the can do list was go to Church, tithe, give offerings, witness, read your Bible, and pray. Throw in a potluck now and then, have a good life, and wait until Jesus comes back. But Jesus didn't go through all that He went through so we could be busy with religious activities. He placed the Spirit of resurrection within us that we might conquer something.

Most have an Old Testament view of holiness in a New Testament era—and the eras are completely different. The Old Testament was to prepare humanity for a Savior—not just to prepare them to receive one, but to prepare them to ask for one. The Law and the Prophets continually exposed requirements from God that people could not keep. But grace came along and changed everything. You can't do enough stuff to make yourself clean before God. We are in desperate need of a Savior and even now, 2,000 years later, it is vital we live with that consciousness—that we cannot work hard enough to get God's favor. We have His favor, and we must live from that favor to increase what we already have.

It's a strange concept in the Kingdom. You actually get more of what you have by living out of what you have. If you can make that adjustment and learn to live in grace, your conduct changes so much more dramatically than when you try to work to obtain favor.

The prophet Isaiah continues this most beautiful picture of a highway concept.

Go through, go through the gates,
Clear the way for the people;
Build up,
Build up the highway,
Remove the stones,

Lift up a standard over the peoples (Isaiah 62:10 NASB).

I believe the gates in this passage refer to *praise*, as mentioned in Isaiah 60:18. When the people of God give God praise, something happens in the atmosphere. The obstacles of ideologies, culture, and spiritual strongholds are confronted. Continuous praise, that is both sacrificial, and a lifestyle, eventually removes the inferior and establishes a Heaven-like realm over geographical locations. It happens wherever the people of God gather to worship, but eventually it has an effect on entire cities. This heavenly atmosphere changes people's perception of reality. This process is called building a highway. A worshiping community changes the atmosphere over the city that actually gives those who don't know Christ a place of easy access to know Him.

Holiness Manifests in Power

Holiness in character is the manifestation of the power of God on the nature of man. Holiness affects the human body through healing. Holiness demands expression, and that expression is the manifestation of power, giving language to what the Spirit of God is doing. The Lord was "declared to be the Son of God with power according to the Spirit of holiness by the resurrection of the dead" (Rom. 1:4). Miracles, like the resurrection, are a normal expression of holiness.

At times our love for God is measured by that which we hate. He is still the judge and will always condemn whatever interferes with love. How much did God hate sickness? As much as He hated sin. They are dealt with almost as one and the same.

What sin is to my soul, sickness is to my body. He hated sickness enough to allow His Son to experience such a brutal whipping. The blood covers our sin, but the wounds paid for our miracle. That is how much He hates sin and sickness. We cannot be tolerant of those things, because what you tolerate dominates.

Our Commission

Holiness has a transforming effect on all creation as well. Romans 8:22 says that "creation groans for the revealing of the sons and daughters of God." Nature longs to manifest the Kingdom. The earth groans for this, wanting to be healed. Even water longs to be walked on again. While I'm not contending for our trying to create an earthly utopia, I am also not discounting the fact that creation is affected by the manifestation of God's presence upon His people.

What happens in the spirit needs to be measurable in the natural. If you say you love God whom you can't see and you hate your brother whom you can see, then what you are saying is a lie about your love for God (see 1

John 4:20). In other words, what you claim to experience in the unseen realm has to be able to be manifested in the seen realm, or what you claim is in question. He won't let us live with theories that cannot be tested. They've got to be applicable now.

The prophets used natural language to teach of spiritual realities. The desert rejoices in Isaiah 35:1. In verse 2, it blossoms abundantly with joy and singing and the glory of the Lord will be seen. Verses 3 and 4 are the commission: "Strengthen weak hands. Make firm feeble knees. Say to those who are fearful hearted, 'Be strong. Do not fear. Your God will come with vengeance.'"

Run and look for anyone who's faltering and say, "This isn't the time to falter. This is our moment, the moment you were born for. Don't be afraid." Having the right message in the right hour releases an unparalleled realm of supernatural activity. This is Heaven's response to our response to His commission: "Then the eyes of the blind shall be opened and the ears of the deaf shall be unstopped. The lame shall leap like the deer, and the tongue of the dumb shall sing" (Isa. 35:5-6). This is God's "Amen" to our proclaiming the right message. And he uses nature to illustrate the abundant Christian life: "For waters will burst forth in the wilderness, and streams in the desert...."

A Drink Becomes a River

Jesus became sin so that you and I would become the righteousness of God. We became God's righteousness in the earth. He says, "Arise, shine for His light has come," not "Arise and *reflect*"—because once you are touched by light, you *become* light. He says that if we come to Him and drink, out of our innermost being will flow rivers of living water (see John 7:38). So a drink of Him turns your innermost being into a producer of a river whose volume is so much greater than the drink you received. You become a releaser of that very Kingdom that impacted and changed you. Your nature, your being, your person, everything about you, is dramatically shifted in the moment you come into contact with the King and His Kingdom.

The Kingdom culture celebrates what God is doing without stumbling over what God didn't do. We must resist the temptation to build our theology around what didn't happen. The world around us cries for an authentic display of Christ. And we become that answer if we don't stumble over what didn't happen.

We are responsible to seek Him for specific breakthrough in private. Also learn from those who have already experienced the breakthrough you long for. Being in the environment of their ministry releases a grace to do the same. Be ready to receive from those who are outside of your theological preferences, as God often hides His best gifts for us in the most unlikely package, just to ensure we have the necessary hunger and humility to live in the gift once we receive it. Look for the impossible and take the risks necessary to confront it and give opportunity for a miracle.

May God release a Spirit of wisdom and revelation upon His people once again that we might see Jesus more clearly, and that we might re-present Jesus more accurately. In the same way that Moses' face shone with the glory of God after seeing His unlimited goodness, so God wants to change the face of the Church in our generation.

The goodness of God is the cornerstone of our theology: one that must be lived, preached, and demonstrated.

It's all about Jesus, who is perfect theology.

About Bill Johnson

Bill and Brenda (Beni) Johnson are senior pastors of Bethel Church in Redding, California. Bill is a fifth generation pastor with a rich heritage in the things of the spirit. Together they serve a growing number of churches that have partnered for revival. This apostolic network has crossed denominational lines in building relationships that enable church leaders to walk in both purity and power.

The Lord has used Bill to launch a frontal attack against unbelief, complacency, and doubt. Through healings that occur at every meeting, faith has been strengthened and revival fires fanned in the hearts of believers. Bill teaches a life of faith that produces a relationship between the faithful one and the surrendered believer. The power of God reveals His nature and is ushered in by His Presence. Bill believes that teaching truths about God without an encounter leads to spiritual pride. An encounter with God produces both a revelation of God and revelation of self, thus transforming us.

In this present move, God has brought Bill into a deeper understanding of the phrase, "... on earth as it is in heaven." Heaven is the model for our life and ministry. Jesus lived with this principle by only doing what He saw His Father doing. Learning to recognize the Holy Spirit's presence and how to follow His lead enables us to do the works of Christ—destroying the works of the devil. Healing and deliverance must become the common expression of the gospel of power once again.

Bill and the Bethel church family have taken on this theme for life and ministry. Healings, ranging from cancer to broken bones to learning disorders and emotional healing, happen with regularity. This is the "children's bread." and these works of God are not limited to revival meetings. The church is learning how to take this anointing to the schools, workplace, and neighborhoods with similar results. Bill teaches that we owe the world an encounter with God, and that the gospel without power is not the gospel that Jesus preached.

Destiny Image Books By Bill Johnson

God is Good
Hosting the Presence
Hosting the Presence Every Day
When Heaven Invades Earth
The Supernatural Power of a Transformed Mind
Strengthen Yourself in the Lord
Releasing the Spirit of Prophecy
Dreaming with God
Here Comes Heaven
Release the Power of Jesus
The Supernatural Ways of Royalty
Spiritual Java
Walking in the Supernatural
A Life of Miracles
Center of the Universe
Center of the Universe Too
Dream Journal
A Daily Invitation to Friendship with God
Invading Babylon

NOTES